Dare2BU

Debra Simmons

Acknowledgements

Everyone who has ever written a book will know that there are way to many people to thank everyone individually for the part they played in bringing it to fruition.
I have so many people that I am deeply grateful for.
That said I would like to single out a few people who have played a big part in getting this book out of my head and into the world.

My lovely partner Russ who always encourages me to follow my heart and gives the best hugs. Especially on my darkest days.
My two awesome nieces Lucy and Beccy who gave up everything to follow this dream with me. They have read edited and put me right when I was ready to give up.
And the wonderful Jules, who has come on board to help out in any way she could just because she can…you gotta love her.

Dedication

To my amazing children Gemma, Laura and Josh who have taught me way more than they know they have. I am beyond proud of you all.

Table of Contents

Part Three

Part Four

Dare2BU

9

Foreword

I feel honoured and privileged to be asked to write this foreword. I am not famous, I have never written book, and I have not known Deb for years and years and years! I first met Deb in February 2017, and yet it seems like I have never not known her. I walked into the room where she was holding her fortnightly "Great Conversations" and I heard something that night that went on to change my life.

Deb was describing the Three Principles of Mind Thought and Consciousness, and she expertly wove them into her metaphors and analogies of her personal life.

Debra's deep understanding and passion in what she shares about her understanding of the principles is evident in the way she lives her life, the way she speaks and how she writes. Her enthusiasm is palpable and you cannot help but feel, and be affected by, her bubbly and infectious nature.

From our first meeting to the present day, my life has incrementally changed beyond recognition and my deeper understanding of myself has, almost by osmosis, crept into my consciousness.

This is entirely down to listening and being around Deb and attending her talks, workshops, courses and retreats, and watching how she Walks Her Talk regarding this "design for life" as she describes in this book.

This book has been put together from the original 40 day Warrior course written by Deb. Her openness and willingness to share her life stories by way of example allows you to delve deep into your own created reality and seeing her true authentic self, somehow helped me to realise my own true self too. The truth of who we truly are, the creative potential of the Universe. Its page by page revelation gives you the time and space to absorb and reveal this for yourself and will take you on a journey of self-discovery.

Within these pages, what becomes obvious is Debra's unshakable resolute and deep understanding of how the principles describes our design for life and this cannot help but touch you. How this understanding has impacted hugely upon her and her willingness to share her own struggles, empathically draws you in. This book can bring you the freedom from the shackles of thought. The simplicity of understanding the Principles of Mind Thought and Conscious are so exquisitely described in these chapters and Debs presentation of them I find unique, immensely understandable and profoundly effective. I feel blessed to have her in my life.

If you truly want to live the life you love and discover another way of seeing the world "out there" read on. A whole new world of infinite possibilities awaits you.

Julie Weeks BSc(Hons)
July 2018

Dare2BU

Dare2BU

Written by Debra Simmons

Dare2BU

Introduction

This book is written in the style of a 40-day course, aimed at helping you create the best version of you. Thriving in life is the aim of the game. Why settle with just surviving?
We are going to explore just how amazing you are and how easy it actually is to create an awesome life, doing more of the things you love. When we thrive in life, and show up as our authentic selves it benefits us and this ripples out in the world, thus benefitting and gifting all.
Daring to be you, is where it all begins!

Through a simple, yet deeply profound understanding of how life is being created behind the scenes, for every single one of us, we naturally begin to create more love and beauty in the world.
Life is a gift we are blessed with.

We recommend you read a day or 2 at a time, no more, to allow it to sink in slowly.

Dare2BU

Debra Simmons

Part One;

Debra Simmons

Day 1 – Let's Get Started

Welcome to your dare2bu journey

Let's Get Started

I want to get straight in here with some great news…

Being you and thriving in life is way easier than you think.

This is always true whatever your circumstances.

I'm going to share more about this during our time together, so you can see it for yourself and start to have a life you really love living. I don't want you to simply take my word for it I want you to find this out yourself.

Sometimes it can take a while for us to really see the truth of who we are and for it to sink in. I know from experience, that consistently looking in this direction is a massive help. I'm thrilled you have decided to give yourself the gift of 40 days doing just that. I can't wait to see what happens for you.

I'd like to share with you my motivation behind creating the dare2bu journey and my hopes and dreams for the future for all of us.

There was an awful long time in my life that I didn't do very well. I was anxious and insecure. I felt like I was useless, and it was all happening to me. I had no idea what I could do to change things. I was stuck and felt helpless.

Then I came across this understanding that I am sharing here with you and it changed everything for me.

I had a massive shift when I heard something very deeply. Since then as I continue investigating 'me' I have been continuing to have shifts and my experience of life just gets better and better.

I'm not saying I never feel sad or that I never struggle, I am saying that understanding the truth of who I am and the system I have been born into helps me have a much easier time of being human. Sometimes it seems that my circumstances are great and sometimes not so much, either way how I see and experience life has changed forever and very much for the better.

I would love for everyone to see this, I believe that it will happen, and that the world will be a better place for us all to live in because of that.

It seems that as human beings we have this idea that we know how things are supposed to happen. Then if it doesn't work like that for us we think we are stuck and there is nothing else that we can do.

It looks as if our choices are limited and we can exhaust them and run out of options.

I have seen that this simply isn't true and that once we connect to the truth of who we are it becomes more and more obvious to us that life's options are infinite.

It turns out we are a part of the creative essence of this entire universe. There are simply no limits on that and no limits on our choices.

If all that sounds a bit simple, 'airy fairy' and as if it can't apply to normal everyday stuff like parenting, earning money, relationships and whatever it is you struggle with, I am excited for us to get stuck into our time together because you will begin to see that it is exactly these things that begin to change as you see something for yourself.

For now, I would love you to look at this again.

It turns out you are a part of the creative essence of this entire universe. There are simply no limits on that and no limits on you.

Whether you've heard this a million times before or if it's new to you I invite you to sit with the possibility of it being true, you don't have to believe it, just don't dismiss it out of hand.
If it feels good and you are already OK with this, great. If you need a little more time with it then that's great too, don't worry, never try to know what you don't know or believe anything unless it makes sense to you to do that.

I hope you have enjoyed our opening chapter and introduction, until you pick me up again, be kind and gentle with yourself.

Debra Simmons

Day 2 - Security And Insecurity

Hello and welcome back

I wanted to talk to you today about something that I have spent a lot of time trying to create in my life and it's likely that you have too.

The thing that I'm talking about is **security…**

Well I have some news for you, and it is likely nobody has told you this before. If they did, you probably didn't realise the truth and implications of what they were saying.

You can't create security ~ nobody can, it simply doesn't work that way.

Security is innate.
That means you were born with it, you already have it and nothing or anyone can ever take it away from you.

Security doesn't come from money.
Security doesn't come other people.
Security doesn't come from things.
Security doesn't come from good health.

The only place that security ever comes from is within you.

Not from a physical place inside you but from that creative essence of the universe. That is what you are made from. Security is already there in you it's a part of who you are.

I sooooo wish someone had told me that years ago. It would have saved me lots of heartache and pain.

'That's all very well' I hear you say 'but what does this mean in real terms, in my life, how does that make any difference to me? And are you sure?'

First off - yes, I'm more than sure, I'm certain in fact.

Here's an example… when my son was small he had a teddy bear and an old t-shirt of his dads that he used to like holding on to.
When we put him to bed at night if he hadn't got his teddy and t-shirt there would be no getting him to settle at all.
But as soon as he was tucked up with them he would go to sleep.
He felt secure when he had them and insecure without them.

Now we all know that security doesn't come from a teddy bear or an old t-shirt. But my son never saw that. To him it felt as if his security did come from those things.

As we get older the teddy and the t-shirt are replaced by other people and money and houses and health. We begin to think we are not safe without these things. We are like my son, we simply don't see that security doesn't come from these things.

But the truth is security can't jump from a teddy bear or a car or another person into you.
If you have ever felt secure in your life, and I'm pretty sure you have, then the only place it could have come from is within you.

The difference with knowing that, allows us to begin to see that we always have security within us, and then it starts to be more obvious to us, it shows up for us in places we never expected to feel it.

There's nothing we have to do but see that we have it and then the magic of the system that we are a part of…the intelligent creative essence of the universe…kicks in and life expands to meet our new understanding.

'So if security is innate and I already have it where does insecurity come from, how come I have that too'?

Insecurity is all made up by thought.

Once you have had an insecure thought you are in the insecure thinking club…it could happen again at any time.

But all we need to do is understand what thought is and what it isn't, know it's nature and let the creative intelligence work its magic and rise to meet our new understanding.

27

More about that tomorrow…
In the meantime notice where you are insecure and see
what you have used as your 'teddy bear'

Until the next chapter....

Dare2BU

Day 3 - The Principle Of Thought

Let's talk about thought.

I said yesterday that we would look a little more deeply at thought, what it is and what it isn't....

Thought is a divine gift.

Thought is an energy that passes through us and gives us an experience of life.
It's through the divine energy of thought that we are able to have an experience. All experience is born through thought.

Thought and feeling can't be separated, because they are simply different ways of experiencing the same energy.
Or as another example – 2 sides of the same coin. We can't experience a feeling without having a thought.

Sometimes we feel things but are unaware of having any thinking at all. Sometimes we are thinking deeply but barely notice any particular feelings we are having. Sometimes if feels like we have both thoughts and feelings powering through us.

All of this and any combination of this happens to us because we are blessed with the divine gift of thought **and all we are ever experiencing** is its energy as it passes through.

All thought comes from the creative intelligence of the universe, the same place we come from. It's made of the same stuff we are made from.

The principle of thought is empty.

It's a pure energy that holds the possibility of **everything…but is nothing…**it's simply the source from where all thought and all things come.

We are all connected to this same source, the principle of thought is the same for everyone.

As that empty energy comes into our head it could become **anything** because we can have a thought about absolutely anything.
And it becomes millions of different things…it becomes the personal thoughts you have and the personal thoughts I have. This is different for every one of us.
All seven billion of us have different thinking, it can overlap but it's not exactly the same. As soon as a thought appears in our head it's already created our experience in that moment.

No other person in existence has the exact same thinking as you do.
No other person has the exact same experience that you do.
You are unique.

Ten things you might not know about thought...

1. Just because a thought comes into your head it doesn't mean it's true.
2. Just because a thought comes into your head it doesn't mean you have to think it.
3. You don't have to believe any thought that you have EVER if you don't want to.
4. You don't have to act on any thoughts you have either, not if you don't want to.
5. You don't have to take on other people's thoughts or beliefs.
6. Your mind is your own and it's free.
7. No thought can separate you from the divine intelligent essence of who you are, it's simply not possible.
8. You are always going to have a new thought at some point.
9. With every new thought comes a new reality.
10. Any thought that limits you can't be true ~ You are the creative intelligence of the universe, there are no limits on that.

I invite you to look again at that last one ….

Any thought that tells you that you are limited simply can't be true, because you are the creative essence of the universe.

How often have you had a limiting thought about yourself and believed it to be true?

Way too often I'm going to guess. I know I often have them.
I love that I don't have to believe them.
I love that I don't have to think them.
And I love that I can look to the possibility that I am limitless.
I love that you are no different to me in all of this…you get to do the same… but only if you want to.

Debra Simmons

Day 4 - Separate Realities

Hello and welcome to day 4

Have you ever done something crazy or stupid in your life?
I know I have.

If we want to be compassionate towards others and understand why they do crazy things that make no sense to us and why we can sometimes do crazy things too, then it's really helpful to understand how our reality is created.

That's what we've been beginning to look at for the past few days.

Everything that we see, hear, smell, touch or taste is happening exactly like it is because of the way that the uncontrollable power of thought is showing up in us in that moment.
Reality is created via the principle of thought.

Have you ever heard it said that we all live in separate realities?

I used to think what that meant was that we all saw the same thing differently…

What I have come to realise is that it actually means that in this very moment you and I are both constructing and experiencing our own personal reality. Yours is not the same as mine and they are both in a constant state of change.

You will be experiencing the power of thought as it passes through you and I will be experiencing it as it passes through me.

Reality is not happening to us. It is created through us 100% of the time.

As our thoughts change, so does our reality.

When we get caught up in a headful of unhelpful thinking then our senses will make up a hostile and unfriendly world.
As all that thinking passes then our senses will make up a lighter and brighter friendlier world.

This is happening to all of us, continually.

We can't control any of it, it's just what's happening. But we are often tempted to try and take control.
We even try to convince others that our personal point of view is the right one because it looks like this is the way for us to have a better experience.

Have you ever noticed that sometimes even when something looks very clear and obvious to you, others just can't see it?

This is because what you are experiencing can't be experienced by anyone else, we can only ever experience what thought gives us in that moment. We can't force or even gently pass our reality onto someone else. They will see what they see, until they don't.

Here's the thing, taking control is not the answer nor is convincing others that what we think is the truth. That just gives us a whole lot of stuff to do, clogs our mind with unhelpful thinking and gets in the way of a perfect system doing what it does best, creating reality.

But there is a way to naturally have the best experience available in any given moment.
And that is to understand how our reality is created. Somehow, by simply understanding, unhelpful thinking seems to dissolve all on its own. We are able to be more compassionate to others and with ourselves, to experience more freedom of mind and have fun.

The less unhelpful thinking we are having the clearer our mind becomes and from a clear mind love, compassion and understanding are our natural state. Life feels good.

Have a lovely day :)

Until the next chapter....

Debra Simmons

Day 5 - Let's Re-Cap

Hello, how wonderful to be here with you again…

Let's just look back at what we have covered so far…

Being you and thriving is way easier than you think. It doesn't depend on anything outside of you being a certain way…ever.
Your own default setting is peace, love and wisdom, with everything you need to live and thrive included in the package.

Security comes fitted as standard, you don't have to go and get it from anywhere…other people, money, cars, houses or anything else. Security doesn't come from any of these things. It's something you were born with and you can never lose it. You can relax and breath; you already have it.

Thought is an energy that passes through us and we have an experience of that.
We don't control our thinking, but understanding it as best we can, as if by magic, lightens and lifts our experience of life.

Thought holds all the possibility of everything and it has been gifted to us, so we can experience things beyond our wildest dreams whilst always knowing that we are safe and secure.

No-one else is you… nobody has your thoughts or feelings or experience. You do what you do because of the thinking you are having and believing in that moment, so does everyone else. You don't have to try and make people see what you see, they can't anyway, no more than you can see what they see.
Understanding means that natural compassion and love for each other will happen without you having to do anything other than just be you.

You are unique, and you are built to live and thrive, here, right now in this moment…with nothing needing to be different.

Have a great day
Remember your unique awesomeness

Dare2BU

Day 6 - Let's Have Some Fun!

Let's take a break and have a bit of fun today. Life is made for having fun... how do you have fun?

I love to write poems. Here's one I wrote for you.

It's ALL thought...

Do you know what isn't true?
I will share it here with you

No matter what it is we're taught
The only thing we feel is thought.

There is no circumstance in life
That has the power to cause you strife

When you feel you're missing out
That's just a thought that's causing doubt

When you struggle and feel low
It's pesky thought that's thrown a blow

When all your confidence is gone
That's thought again it's off on one.

It's not all bad I'm glad to say
Cause life was meant to work this way

Dare2BU

YOU are more than thought alone
It cannot stop you on its own

Once you understand and see
There's something more to you and me

We are made of clever stuff
And we will always be enough

Every thought you ever knew
That put a limit onto you

Was simply lying to your face
Now you can put it in its place!

Your human form is built to do
All it is YOU need to do.

YOU lack nothing that you need
Go live this life and go succeed.

Have a great day
Until the next chapter....

Debra Simmons

Day 7 - Get Curious

Hello again, and what a lovely day it is today.

I hope you had a nice day yesterday and enjoyed the fun poem.

I don't know about you, but I love curiosity ~ I think it saved my life.

Let me explain...

Before I came across this understanding that I am sharing with you here, I was scared of life. I didn't think I had what it took to be good at it. I thought one way or another I would always fail because that's what I'd always done.

As I began to understand how our experience is created via thought in the moment from the inside out I started to see I had misunderstood and I realised that there was nothing wrong with me.

Things began to make sense.
The logic of it all fitted with how my life had been and the answer to how to have a different, better experience became clearer.

It may or may not have come as a surprise to you to find out that you, like me, are the creative essence of the universe and there is nothing wrong with you either, whatever experience you are having right now, whether you would call it good or bad.

We are not the experience itself, we are what's underneath that experience, the foundation on which that experience stands.

We are untouchable by experience.

There is something built into the knowing of this that frees our mind and allows us to live a more expanded life. We can have more fun and feel more love and connection. Whether we know it or not that is what we all want in some form or another from life. Everything we do is because we want to feel more love and connection and be happy.

When this happened for me I got curious.

Just knowing how the system worked began to free my mind. It looked like I had more options in places – it had never looked that way before.

So, I started to look for that more. Then in the places that still looked rock solid and unchangeable I would become curious and be open to other possibilities.

The funny (or maybe great) thing is the more we look for truth the more we find it. That's built into the system.

I would find myself in the middle of a situation I didn't like, maybe a friend would let me down when we were supposed to be getting together, or I would get stuck in traffic and be late for an appointment and I would be feeling upset, angry or stupid. Suddenly it would occur to me to get curious and see what else was available to me.

That would take me straight to what was underneath my experience and back to knowing I am always ok because no experience ever changes the truth of who I am.
From here my mind opens up and things begin to happen that I would never have thought were possible before. I see things, ways to be and things to say that just never looked like they were there before.

All of this is available to you too, there is nothing different about how we work!.
You have a connection to the creative essence that is yours, you have your own wisdom. It's built into the system.

I love that you are here and getting curious about how life truly works, about how the experience you are having right now reading this is happening for you.
Keep getting super curious about that. Look for the truth of all experience and your mind will open and you will have your own insights about things in your life that are helpful and personal to you.

That's the magic of this it's both impersonal because it is the same for all of us and it is extremely helpful on a personal level because what occurs to us when we are ready to listen is exactly what we need in that very moment. It's built into the system. Have a fabulous and super curious day.

Debra Simmons

Day 8 - It's Built Into The System

It's good to be here with you again.

Yesterday, I said a few times that 'it's built into the system'.
One of the things that I have seen since I began to understand where my experience actually comes from is that there is way less for me to do because an awful lot of things that I used to think were down to me are actually built into the system.

There is a "pre-existing logic" or "system behind life". It was there before you or I were born and will be there long after we are gone.

It just does it's thing and we don't have to do anything to make it happen, we don't have to believe in it or attract it or repeat affirmations or behave in a certain way, we don't have to be grateful or loving or spiritual or accept anything. We don't even have to like our self or care about anyone else.

There is simply nothing we have to do for it to be totally on our side, for it to guide us and continually be bringing us back to the truth of who we are.

My guess is that you are doing way more than you need to be. Most of us get exhausted by life and make ourselves ill trying so hard to control life or create a whole heap of things we simply have no business messing with.

You can relax and trust the system
Everything you could ever possibly need to have a life you love is already built in

- **Love is built in**
- **Resilience is built in**
- **Confidence is built in**
- **Acceptance is built in**
- **Gratitude is built in**
- **Freedom is built in**
- **Security is built in**

When you look you will find that everything that you could ever possibly need to live in peace and harmony are already built into the system.

Our 'job' is to wake up to, or learn to understand, this system. That's exactly what we are doing here. Simply by doing this we will naturally begin to see we are a part of it's natural flow. Life begins to make sense and we begin to thrive in ways we never imagined were possible.

Life only works in one way. **From the inside out.**
There's nothing we can do to change that, it is fixed that way, which believe me is a very good thing.

The only thing that ever gets us into trouble is that we don't see this and we act as if the system works in ways it never will. We try and change it - which is about as effective as trying to make rain go back up when it's falling down.

Understanding, is the realisation of the perfection of this kind caring beautiful system that we are blessed to be a part of.

It is deeply 'seeing' that although it may not look to us as if everything is ok, it always is.
It is truly 'seeing' that what we think we know from our tiny vantage point makes us feel things should be different to the way they are. It is an innocent misunderstanding on our part.

Don't get me wrong, misunderstanding is perfectly normal, it's human, and it's always okay. Through **understanding** we won't stop being human but, we will know we are always safe and secure and it's fine to be human. It's fine to temporarily forget how life works and get lost in it for a while. That's all part of the fun we can have.

So, go and enjoy being you, it's what you were born to do.
You are whole, complete and perfect as you are right now.
But for your thinking you would know that.

See you again very soon

Debra Simmons

Day 9 - The Inside Out Nature Of Life

Hello there again lovely reader :)

I love that we are here together again today, and I hope you are loving this book so far.
It truly is my passion to share this with you…

Yesterday I said that life only works in one way.
From the inside out.

I wanted to share a bit more about that with you today, to make it a little bit clearer what it is I mean by inside out.

Let's first look at what inside means…inside is quite simply the creative essence of the universe or God.

If you don't like those words then just use another one, the universal energy, the power behind life, higher power, spirit, soul, anything you like, it really doesn't matter. You choose. Just so long as you are clear what I am pointing to…the formless energy from which everything in form (the outside) is created.

So what about outside….obviously, as I just said anything that is in form is the outside…like circumstances, other people, stuff, money, the future, the past. All pretty straight forward I'm guessing and what you were expecting (hopefully).

BUT this one may surprise you! Also included in this list is **YOU.**
Yes that's right. You, the person reading this right now.

Your behaviour, your health, your beliefs, your body, your mind, your brain, your values, your personality, all of it, anything that is YOU…it's all in the form so that means it's on the outside. YOU are outside.

So, what does it mean then when I say life works from the inside out and you are on the outside?

It means that you are not inside and everything else is outside.
It means you are on the outside too. You are part of the world of form and that means you are also 100% created and projected from the inside, from God or the creative essence of the universe…

This means that it's the creative essence of the universe or God, or whatever you choose to call it that decides on your thinking, your mood, your mind-set, your successes, your failures, your ups, your downs, the whole lot of it… None of it is down to you.

The misunderstanding is that you are the one in charge, that it's all on you. That's what has us working so hard and tying ourselves in knots, trying to be and do everything.

It just doesn't work that way.

Once we see this and start to do what is ours to do, enjoying the ride, life becomes a whole lot easier and more fun and we get the best human experience available. We can take our eyes off the road and enjoy the scenery. And when we forget and grab the wheel it's ok, that's normal, we all do it.

Life can be fun from the driver's seat from time to time, driving on a nice summers day, with the window down, the wind in your hair, and the radio playing a merry tune, it's a great experience.
It's just good to remember when the road gets blocked and it is difficult to navigate then we don't need to stay at the wheel. We can rely on the fact that at some point we will remember and just let go again.

Let that settle for a while. It might be a lot to take in.

Don't worry if it makes no sense right now, or you are confused.
That's all good. Nobody can ever truly understand this. But from confusion comes clarity. We can get a feel for the truth of who we are and the proof shows itself when our life, the stuff on the outside starts to get better. We begin to feel more mentally stable and happy and not really for any particular reason necessarily.
Relax and enjoy your day....

Debra Simmons

Day 10 – The Truth Behind Experience

Good morning, afternoon, evening or whatever time it is as you are reading this, it's good to see you here again, not least because it's a really great idea to stay in this conversation.

The time between reading this book is also very important. It's good to just let this settle and go about your day, that way it kinda seeps into your life. Which is exactly what we want to happen.

You may already be noticing changes happening.

Don't worry if you're not. It could be that you just haven't noticed, changes can be very subtle.
Either way be patient, you are on the right track. Which is great news.

Yesterday we looked at the fact that you aren't in control of your thinking, your moods, your mind-set, your successes, your failures, your ups your downs, any of it… None of it is down to you.

Because none of it is down to you it's pointless trying to 'fix' any of it.

This is a big thing for some of us…we soooooo want to 'fix' things both for ourselves and for the people we love. I really know that one because I am exactly the same, I totally want to jump in and make sure everything is always happy and the way I think it should be for my nearest and dearest.

It's so tempting and really looks like a good idea if you or someone you care about is feeling anxious or upset or struggling to try and make it better, to try and fix things and make it right again.

But here's the thing it simply doesn't work that way.

Trying to 'fix' things is pointless at best and can be harmful if we persist.

The blunt truth here is that nothing you experience is real. It's pointless trying to fix something that's not real.

Let me share an example with you to help you see what I'm saying.

Let's say Laura, my daughter, comes home feeling really upset.
She's had a very bad day at work and is feeling like she's made a mistake starting her new job. It looks like the management are rubbish at the new place. Some people have walked out because it's so bad and she is really worried about how it will all affect her.
She is getting more and more upset, angry and frustrated and it really looks like the management are causing her to feel that way.

58

What if I told you that Laura isn't having an experience of the management and they are nothing to do with how she is feeling?

The truth is she isn't, and they are not.

How can that possibly be the case?

Well here's the thing, outside of our ability to have an experience nothing exists.
Think about it, have you ever had an experience that was outside of your awareness.

To put it another way - no thought, no experience.

No thought means no management. They simply don't exist unless you have an experience of them.

That means it's not possible for the management to be causing anyone to feel anything. It can only ever come from the energy of thought or our ability to have an experience, which are one and the same thing.

All experiences in life are always a projection from inside to out.

Understanding what's truly going on makes it the best fun to play in these experiences and be the best person we can be within them. That's the game of life.
But it all gets very messy when we forget that is what's happening and treat them as if they are real.

So, it's really beneficial for us to know the truth, and not to try and fix any experience however tempting it gets.

The answer is always to gently point our self back to the truth.

We won't always remember it in every second, but it's a great foundation to come back to when things get a bit sticky out there in the world of experience.
Once you start to know it you will begin to find it naturally occurring to you when you need it most. You can trust this system, but only 100% and only always.

Have a nice day,
Be soft, gentle and kind to yourself.

Dare2BU

Debra Simmons

Part Two;

Dare2BU

Day 11 - Relax And Reflect

Hello again!

We've covered a lot of ground in the last 10 days and some of what I've shared may have hit hard against what you have believed to be true for a very long time, this can shake life up a bit.
So just breathe, take a moment and allow yourself space to just be where you are right now. Give yourself that gift for today.

I want to share a quote I love with you;

"Life is like any other contact sport, you may encounter hardships of one kind or another. Wise people find happiness not in the absence of such hardships but in their ability to understand them when they occur."
        ~ SYD BANKS

It doesn't look to me as if we get to choose what is going to happen to us in life. Life is going to ebb and flow. That's the way it works.

We are blessed by the gift of experience.
We are built to live life
We are built to enjoy it.
We are built to withstand knocks and bumps.
We are built to bounce back.

When we look to understand how our experience is created, the magic in the system kicks in and life becomes lighter, easier and more enjoyable.

Debra Simmons

Day 12 - The Difference That Makes The Difference

Good day to you....

I am often asked if I still get scared about things and if I still feel fear and insecurity.
Well the short answer is yes, I do.
But the thing that has made the difference to me is knowing that just because I'm feeling scared and insecure about something it doesn't mean that it's true. Or that I need to react to my thinking. It isn't telling me about something fixed and real in the world.

The difference that makes the difference is that I understand the nature of thought now in a way I never did before.

Thought is the creative energy of the universe and I feel it as it passes through my system. Sometimes that feeling can be very strong indeed - so strong it's hard not to believe that it's giving me information about something independent of my thinking.

At some point I always remember that there simply isn't anything independent of my thinking.

This happens because *I know it's true.*

At this point I'm being orientated back towards truth and I'm already starting to self-right. I'm already beginning to see that thought can't take away from who I truly am and it doesn't render me useless just because it's giving me a full on felt experience.

You are just like me, we work in the same way, understanding will point you back to truth and to automatically self-righting when thought is doing it's full on funky stuff.

Have a lovely day....

Dare2BU

Day 13 - The Principle Of Mind

Hello again, what a wonderful morning.

I'm glad that you are still here reading this book, I know that in our busy lives it can often feel as if there are millions of things vying for our attention and it can be easy to discard reading because we have so much to do.

I'm glad you haven't.

The reason this book is done in this way and we are exploring the same thing in each chapter is because, being drip-fed in this way, deepens our understanding. Being in the conversation every-day,gently and continually orientated towards truth does something for us. Even if it's so subtle that we don't always notice it happening.

Thank you for still being here.

I wanted to share something about the principle of mind with you today, although those amongst you who are observant will have noticed that a thread of mind is running through everything I am writing.

Mind is the God principle.
The energy or power of life itself.

The kind creative essence of the universe.

It is through the power of mind that all of the infinite possibility of life comes to us as human beings in the form of thought.
It is through the kindness that's built into the system that we get to experience the full-on nature of life and yet always have that place of peace to come back to.

We are made from this creative power and we can learn to understand it's nature and thrive in life or we can misunderstand its nature and, to the degree we misunderstand, we will struggle and see life as hard and unforgiving.

There is nowhere in life that we need to fall short of thriving. When we believe the thinking we have that, tells us we are limited, then we will experience limitations, struggle and hardship.

No thought that tells you that you are limited is ever true.
You never have to believe a limiting thought again.

It's not within our power to control life.
But because we are the creative essence of the universe we don't need to.
That is the job of Mind. It is way above our pay grade.
We can let go of control and play full out, that is our job.
Mind gives us possibility, creativity and capability.

With these things we can chose to create anything, just because we can. Just because we are here, and we are alive.

71

It's not that everything we choose to create will always turn out the way we want it to, it's not that we will always get everything our own way, I don't know anyone whose life is like that.

Most of us do what we do in order to be secure or free or happy or at peace. Magic starts to happen when we see that we already have all of these things and we don't need anything to go the way we think it should to get them. Mind gives us these things unconditionally and then we get to live our life the way we chose to.

With this understanding we can chose to create anything, just because we can. Just because we are here and we are alive.

Have a beautiful and creative day....

Dare2BU

Day 14 - You Never Have To Believe Any Thought You Have

Hello
It's good to be here with you again,

I wanted to share two things with you today that I was thrilled about when I realised they were true and what that meant about how I lived my life. I mentioned them yesterday but today I want you to look more closely at them and consider the implications of seeing the truth of them for yourself.

1) You never have to believe any thought that tells you you are limited, ever again.

2) No thought can change the truth of who you are. It's just not possible.

You have my permission to simply not believe any limited thinking that ends up in your head. You can ignore it. You can just get on with being capable and creative and full of all the possibility that life has to offer no matter what's going on in your head.

It seems to me we get way too hung up on the thought that's in our head. We let it become out master and believe it has power over us.

That is just NOT so!

Have you ever been told that you have to change your thinking or overcome or get rid of limiting beliefs? Have you ever been told that you need to change your mind-set to be able to make money, have a great relationship, love your job…or any other thing you may want to do or be in your life?

If you have then I have news for you ~ **You don't**

Yesterday we looked at the principle of Mind. We are made from Mind and Mind contains possibility, creativity and capability and so do you.

There is nothing you have to do about your thinking, you don't have to change it or overcome it, you can let it be there doing whatever it is doing, you can choose to ignore it.

Yep it's that simple, it's only the fact that we have never really looked at this as a possibility that we have managed to overlook the fact that we can do this and that it's way easier than you might think.

The thing about thought is that it's all made up. Yep that's right, **ALL** of it. You don't have to listen to it or believe it.

There will always be something else on offer if you don't stick with what you're thinking in that moment.

I want to share a real-life example of this with you.

Russ, my partner, had been working away for quite a while, so we hadn't spent time together for a bit. The morning after he got back I wanted us to go out for breakfast together. He had other things on his mind and didn't want to go.

My thinking kicked in and told me that if he loved me he would want to spend time with me as much as I wanted to spend time with him. After all we hadn't seen each other for quite a while.
In that moment, it looked and felt very real and very true to me.

I was really getting into the story and I was starting to get upset and be quite off with Russ. We were headed for an argument when it occurred to me that maybe I was just feeling the energy of thought as it passed through me.

That was all it took.

The hold that the energy had on me had loosened enough for me to stop believing the story I was telling myself and we were back on solid ground.
The crisis had passed.
I knew I didn't want an argument and that there was nothing going on that we needed to fall out over.

I know that both Russ and I are connected to Mind and the more I look in the direction of what that means for me then the better my life experience becomes in all areas.

New thought is always available to us, knowing that is a game changer. We are never stuck with anything.

Dare2BU

I have a challenge for you tomorrow....

Debra Simmons

Day 15 - Lets Play

If you have ever met me, you will know that I just love having fun!
I think it's way too easy to get into the habit of taking life far too seriously.
It seems to me we are here to discover ourselves, to wake up to the truth of who we are, and I can't think of a better way to do that than through play.

Children learn to walk and talk and all of the fundamental things they need to survive in life through play, it's only when we get to the point where we think it's time to take life seriously that we come unstuck.

So, I would love you to approach today's challenge as a playful adventure and let's see what we can learn together.

Yesterday I gave you permission to simply not take any notice of any limiting thinking that ends up in your head. Your challenge, should you choose to accept it, is to ignore all limiting thoughts for the next 24 hours.

How many of you screamed out "that's impossible". All sorts of thinking, once it's there in your head, is causing havoc, being loud and disruptive and demanding attention ~ It can't just be ignored.

If you did some version of that then you just had your
first limiting thought that you are allowed to ignore…
you are already off to a great start.

You see one of the things that I discovered, when I came
across the principles, is that thought wants to take us in
one direction and that our peace of mind is in the
OPPOSITE direction.

Another thing I discovered is that thought is very good at
disguising itself. Pretending to be something way more
important than it is; Truth.

So, for the next 24 hours I am inviting you not to go in
the direction that thought wants to take you.
I am inviting you to have a go at seeing through some of
the disguises that your thinking has been wearing.

It's a fun game and one that has given me a lot of peace
in my life.

Like all games we don't always get the hang of it straight
away, so don't worry if you are not great at it, taking part
is enough right now.
So, let's give it 24 hours and see what occurs to you in
that time.

Have some fun with this - it's a game

Dare2BU

Day 16 - You Are Not Your Thinking

How did you get on with our challenge?
I hope you had fun.

I had a new client, I went to her house, somewhere I've never been before. I drove to a strange address and parked up. I walked up to the door and knocked.
Nothing.
I waited and knocked again.
Nothing.
I rang the bell and knocked and waited.
Nothing.
My thinking was going crackers.
"You got the address wrong"
"You are pathetic",
"You messed up the time"
"Runaway, maybe nobody saw you at the door"

And other rubbish that my thinking sometimes throws at me.

Then I remembered this challenge and just left the thinking alone.

I ignored it and took no notice of it at all. I reminded myself that it's just energy that I don't control. It wasn't sharing anything helpful or true with me. I immediately began to feel better.

I got my phone out of my bag with the intention of calling the lady and my thinking started again. Have you noticed how thinking does that?
'She won't want you calling her"
"She's probably ignoring you on purpose because she doesn't want to talk to you"
"Just walk away, know when you're beaten."

So, I just ignored it and rang the lady.

She answered straight away.
She then went on to really apologise and say how sorry she was that she hadn't heard the door.
I went into the house with a clear head knowing that both she and I are the creative energy of the universe and that nothing could change that, no thought has that power.
We ended up having a fabulous session and arranging another time to meet.

I love knowing that I never have to believe my thinking.
I love knowing that all experience is just thought in the moment.
I love knowing that the only 'job' I have in all this is to understand.
That's a part time job, not the full-time job plus overtime I used to do!

I don't have to control my thinking
I don't have to be scared of my thinking.
I don't have to control the world and everything in it.

I love knowing that my ability to cope with anything is never compromised by my thinking. **I can think it is** but that's the funny thing about it, I also know that's just another limiting thought that I don't have to believe and that I have permission to ignore.

This is a harmless example of what thought can be like. Understanding that we all have this stuff, or some version of it, going on in our head and that we can just ignore it means we can get on with just being great in life.

Somehow the more we do this the quieter and less convincing the limiting thinking gets.
It's only when we misunderstand and think what is in our head is real and true and must be listened to that we come unstuck

If you want to carry on playing our game then be my guest....
Until tomorrow have a great day whatever you are doing.

Dare2BU

Day 17 - Life Is A Full On Experience

Hello again

I hope you are well and enjoying our time together as much as I am?

On day 15 I said that thought wants to take you in one direction and that peace of mind is in the other direction. I wanted to share a bit more about that with you today.

That statement may sound as if thought is an enemy.
I want to assure you it's not.
Thought is a wonderful gift, one we are lucky to have, if we didn't have the energy of thought passing through us then we wouldn't have any known experience of life.

So, just stop reading for a moment and look around you at something, wherever you are right now, anything, … you know about what you are looking at because you have the gift of thought.

Whatever you love the most in the world…you know about it through the gift of thought.

The sky, the sea, the mountains, food, a cool drink on a hot day…all of it, absolutely everything is known by you through the gift of thought. There simply isn't any way to have an experience outside of thought.

No thought means no experience.

Pain, sadness, hurt, loss you get all that through the gift of thought too. Nothing is left out. We get to have it all a full-on experience of life, no holds barred.

So, why then does thought want to take you away from the truth of who you are?

We experience what we think.

Nothing can change the *fact* of who we are. Peace, Love and Wisdom, the kind creative essence of the universe. But we can think that we are less than that and so have that full-on experience.

If we didn't fall for our thinking in the moment we wouldn't fully experience life like we do.
As the creative essence of the universe we willingly agree to forget who we are to have this full on experience, because we know that it's ok, there's no danger ever. Nothing can ever change the fact of who we are.

When things get a bit overwhelming it's built in that we have the capacity to remember the truth. As soon as we are orientated towards truth we begin to self-right.

Thought wants to gift us the full on no holds barred experience of life.

Our peace of mind lies in remembering the truth of who we are.
We have the capacity through this fabulous system we are a part of to have both, a full-on experience and peace of mind. What could be a better gift than that?

The other thing to be aware of is it really doesn't matter either way, no experience has the capacity to change the truth of who we are. However crazy our mind gets and however turbulent our experience we are always still peace love and wisdom and the ability to create the illusory experience that we are not.

What a great gift understanding is too.

Dare2BU

Day 18 - Metaphors And Paradoxes

Hello again

How are you doing?
I hope you are beginning to know that you are always okay?
Not just know because I have said it, but also know because you have become curious and looked for your own okay-ness and seen that it is, in fact, always there.

I wanted to share with you today how big a part metaphor play in the sharing of this understanding.

It's very easy to get so taken by a metaphor that we forget that's what it is and mistake it for the thing it is pointing us towards – Truth.
At some point a metaphor will break down because it's not truth.

The principles themselves are metaphors.

This understanding of the mind makes sense, it is logical. There is a logic to the mind and the way it works for us.

But it is also spiritual and there is a place that we are pointing towards that can't be talked about in words because there are no words that could hold it.

Well what we are sharing here is the same, it just can't be held within words. All the words I am using are just metaphors or a sign-post, to try and point you towards truth.

No metaphor is ever truth, they are just a way of saying it's like this **but it's not actually this**. It's worth remembering that second part – **"but it's not actually this"** – so as not to get lost in the metaphor itself.

We have a way of understanding truth, of knowing it even though it is beyond words. Another gift we are blessed with that is built into the system that we are.

Our understanding of the truth will be personal to us and helpful to us in ways that only we will see, and yet truth is the oneness of everything, it is where we are all the same.

The paradox of truth is that we are all the same and yet we are all different and individual.
We are always ok, we have everything we will ever need. And yet life is a contact sport.

It is in the embracing of these paradoxes that opens us up to living a full, amazing and beautiful life.

I will be back again tomorrow orientating us both back to the truth of who we are and of life.

Debra Simmons

Day 19 - Are You Sure You Want Control?

How is your day going today?
I wanted to talk to you about the illusion of control.

Before I came across this understanding of how life works, I used to think I was in control of my life. I used to think that making decisions and all that resulted from those decisions, any outcomes and the effort I put into things was all my doing, I was on my own, having to shoulder all of that by myself.

I would think things like "If it's to be it's down to me"

I don't see it like that anymore. I realise that I am a part of the intelligence of the universe. That intelligence is always working through me and for me.

That is a massive relief I can tell you.

You are no different to me, you aren't on your own in life either. The whole thing and how it all works out isn't just down to you.

If you are having doubts and feel as if you want to be in control, master of your destiny, just stop and think about that for a moment.

Imagine every decision being totally yours, every outcome, every move you make has to be worked out entirely by you. Imagine having no intuition or gut feelings, no instinct and no inner knowing to guide you in any way, you have to calculate it all by yourself. Imagine what it would be like if everything was down to you. Imagine all of the things you would have to know to really pull that off!

It is the mistaken belief that we are in control that causes us a lot of pain and confusion.

When I have my weekly meet-ups I often ask people how they ended up in the room. It is amazing how many things have happened that could not have been foreseen or planned so that each person has ended up there on that night.

When we stop to look, all of our lives are full of serendipity and coincidences that are most certainly not within our control.

Finding out the truth of who we are, finding out that everything in life isn't down to us alone brings with it freedom and relief.

Life only works one-way. We aren't in control of some things and not others. We are not separate from the creative intelligence of the universe, we are one with it, and we are always being guided and taken care of.

So, relax and enjoy life.
There's way less to do than you thought.

Dare2BU

Day 20 - The Halfway Mark…

Hello again

I hope you have begun to notice insights happening for you, your mind beginning to open a little and life looking a little different.

We have covered a lot of ground and we have been looking at truth together from many different angles. I would like to do something a little differently today.

I would like to invite you to randomly select a number between one and nineteen, just take the first number that enters your mind whatever it is.

Now find the chapter that corresponds with that number and re-read it.

We are always being guided and nothing happens by accident, it might be interesting to see what you have been guided to look at again.

Have a lovely day,
See you again tomorrow to continue our journey together.

Dare2BU

Part Three;

Dare2BU

Day 21 - Just A Small Reminder Of Your Greatness

Hello...

It's good to be back here with you again today.
I hope your week is going well?

We have been looking together at the truth of who we are and how life works for every single one of us. It's very good for us to be orientated towards truth. When we are orientated towards truth it's built into the system that we begin to self-right. Looking towards truth will do that for you.

I wanted to take a moment today and just remind you of what you have going for you because, if you are anything like me, it's very easy to get into the ups and downs of everyday life and forget just how amazing life is and just how blessed and fortunate we are.

You have a connection to the creative essence of the universe, the power behind life, the power that created everything. The power that is the allness of everything. This is the power that is running the show, and it is what is always guiding and taking care of you in every second of every day. It is running through you in this very moment giving you life.

Our experience of life changes moment to moment and is a reflection of how clear we are about that connection at any given time.

The connection we have can never be broken and never changes, but we have the ability to create the illusion that we are on our own and we can fall for that illusion big time! Our connection always remains, it's only the illusion that makes it appear it has gone.

Knowing this is what is going on, and being reminded of the truth of who we are, is our salvation.

The clearer we see the connection the better our experience.

Note that I didn't say the better our circumstances.

No matter what our circumstances, our experience will always reflect our state of mind. Our experience will always reflect our understanding of our connection to the power of life, the creative essence of the universe or God. It is always enough to Jjust know this is what is happening.

There is often so much going on in the world of form, or all around us, and we get drawn into it. It can really seem to make sense and it's tempting to the best of us to try and alleviate poverty, discrimination, abuse and war by putting things on the outside.

But we simply don't work that way, and never will.

To really be effective in changing these things we have to remember that.

The brilliant thing is that you are reading this so you are one of a relatively small number of people who have stumbled onto the truth.
This is the greatest gift you will ever have, my wish for you is that you don't stop looking in this direction until you have realised the enormity of what you have found here.

Have a day as great as you are.

Dare2BU

Day 22 - Less Work, More Play

Good Morning

When we misunderstand how life works we work way too hard. We do lots of things that we really don't need to do. When we get so taken up and busy doing all of these things we also often miss what is ours to do, which is understand. That's it, that's all we have to do, know who we are and just be that.

It can really feel like we are having to go it alone in life and do it all, that is just not the way this life we have been gifted works.

The more we understand, the more we stop doing things we have no business doing and the easier life becomes. We begin to see how many things are already done for us and how well we are taken care of and we start to recognise what is up to us.

On day 19 when I talked about control, I also talked about the fact that we are powered by the creative essence of the universe. Words fall short of describing exactly what this means but we always have this connection, we are an extension of this power, we are made from it, we are it.

This power is what gives us life. It moves through us as thought. We don't have control over the creative essence of the universe, but we don't have to be scared of it either. We can rest assured that it will always be there for us. If it stopped being there we wouldn't be here either.

The nature of a being human is that our state of mind changes. Thought, or the creative essence of the universe, passes through us and we feel it as it does this. This is what is always happening, nothing else is ever going on.

When we stop feeling the need to be in control we get to play with this creative energy, that's when life really starts to be fun.

Take this morning, I got all in my head about writing this chapter, it needed to be done, it needed to be good and I needed to do it.
I sat and stared at the blank screen.

I wrote a few lines and I deleted them, they weren't right.

The blank screen stared back at me, and so I tried again.
But again, nothing of any use was happening.
I was starting to get frustrated with myself.
I needed to do this, I have other stuff I needed to be getting on with.

I got up and went to get a drink.

While I was at the sink, I remembered that I didn't need to get all caught up and feel so alone and I started to laugh.

The only difficult thing for me now was how I was going to describe how this works without making it sound as is it's a whole load of things that I do that you can copy and have the same results.

That made me laugh too…another limiting thought I can simply ignore, and here, right now as I write this, my fingers are flying over the keys…

Along with the realisation that I didn't need to get all caught up, built into that thought was acceptance, allowing, just being, not getting in my own way, the knowing that this chapter is already a done deal.

That's the power of understanding.

These are all of the things that we talk about 'doing' because it makes so much sense. We know that all of these things are what will give us peace of mind, security and a way better experience of life, the place we go wrong is thinking we need to 'do' all of these things. They are already built into the system and done.

Look to understand, relax and allow, its sooooo much fun to play with this creativity.

I hope you enjoyed this chapter, as much as I enjoyed playing at writing it, as much as I enjoyed those moments of remembering who I am, remembering my true nature. I also know that being human means we are a part of the ebb and flow of life, that's perfectly normal, there's nothing wrong there either and nothing to be scared of.

Have a wonderful day. Looking forward to being here again tomorrow.

Dare2BU

107

Day 23 - The Ebb And Flow of Life

When I first came across the principles that we are looking at together here I had read a few self-help books and heard about positive thinking. I was looking for a way to feel better and have an easier and nicer life. These things seemed like the answer.

There were a lot of things in my life that weren't going the way I wanted them to and it very much looked to me as if I needed things to be different for me to be ok.

What I have come to see more and more clearly lately is that my okay-ness doesn't depend on any of that stuff.

Okay-ness, or peace, or love, or the creative essence of the universe…whatever it makes sense to you to call it, is built into the fiber of who we are, nothing can change that.

Life is meant to ebb and flow. We can't stop it anymore than we can stop the tide going in and out, but that's okay because it's part of the amazing system we are born into. Understanding this will always be enough.

The system works something like this…

We have a build-up of thinking and we feel bad, or upset
or unlovable, then thought falls away and we feel better.
We feel clear and focused.
This happens to every human being and it's not
connected to our circumstances or our surroundings.

All human beings are born with the gift of thought, we
have a personal thought system, we have an intellect and
we can process thoughts.

Our intellect is great, it's really helpful to us & it's
fantastic for working things out when we have all the
pieces of the equation - like a math's problem or booking
a train or what time to leave home to make it to an
appointment.

But when it comes to our spiritual nature our intellect
isn't so great, in fact it does this very unhelpful thing…it
totally makes up a connection between what we feel (the
inside) and what is going on in the world (the outside).
Creating this illusion, making up this connection takes a
whole lot of personal thinking, when this happens by it's
very nature it obscures our connection to the truth of who
we are.

As soon as we stop looking to our intellect for answers
and look inside, which we invariably will at some point,
all of that thought will just fall away. That's the thing
with an illusion - there is no substance to it and it can
disappear in an instant.

This is when we feel lots better, our connection to the
truth of who we are is restored and we are back to being
in balance.

From the moment we are born our thought system is capable of doing this, we will be fooled by the outside-in illusion created by our thinking in the moment and then this thinking falls away, as we look inside for answers.

We are spiritual beings who have found ourselves here in form. The way this works is that thinking builds up, we get fooled by the illusion of thought then it falls away, and we come back to truth. We feel bad, we feel good. The ebb and flow of life.

This is what being human is all about, the dance between our spiritual nature, the truth of who we are and our humanness, the illusion created by thought in the moment.

It's great to be human, we are very blessed and gifted. What makes it even better is when we know how it all works. There is never anything to be scared of, we are always taken care of and we will always keep coming back to the truth of who we are.

Remember whether you are up or down, you are always okay, it's just the ebb and flow of life.

Have a wonderful day.

Dare2BU

Day 24 - You Just Can't Lose

Hello

I cannot count the number of times that people have said something like this to me:

I've lost the principles, I had them for a while but now they've gone again...

Or

I don't think I really understand these principles because they just don't work for me.

Well I would really like to share with you today how neither of these things could ever possibly be true. But it is entirely possible to have an experience of it being true.

If either of these statements sound like something you might think, feel or say then read on because I will explain why it's never possible to lose the principles or for them to stop working for you.

The Principles – Mind, Thought and Consciousness - are a way to describe or to put words to the process that each one of us are born into which gives us our moment to moment experience of being human and being alive.

This process is always happening to everyone it never stops for one second while you are here in this form known as being human and being alive.

You are the principles in action, whether you know it or not, whether you believe it or not, whether you are happy sad, good, bad, up, down, thriving or messing up. You can't get away from being the principles any more than you can get away from yourself. Wherever you go there you are and there is this process in action creating your experience.

The principles are not a way of describing how to have a better life.
But it turns out that a by-product of understanding how we work and what is truly going on when we experience life is that we do find peace, freedom and the best human experience available.
That's why understanding is where your salvation lies.

Sometimes understanding can be a bit of a slippery fish and we can appear to lose something we thought we knew. But that's just a natural part of the ebb and flow of life we talked about yesterday.

One of the principles …Thought…is very good at grabbing our attention and appearing to be something it's not…ultimate truth.

In any moment you can have any thought and depending on how clear your connection to the truth of who you are is in that moment that thought will appear to be anything from 100% independent truth (which it absolutely is not) to 100% creative energy passing through (which it absolutely is).

113

When our thoughts seem to be 100% independent truth then we are having an experience of struggling in life. When we know they are 100% creative energy passing through then our experience will be one of peace, love and wisdom.

It's this knowing that can be hidden to us via the thinking we are having in any moment, obscured like the sun behind the clouds

The more we understand, the more we can have any thinking and still know the truth.
We can't change our thinking or control it, but we can understand it and that is always enough.

The truth can't be changed by anything ~ our experience can.
We will always be peace, love and wisdom.
The extent to which we experience that can vary wildly depending on our level of understanding in any moment.

The depth to which we can understand is infinite.
We will never reach the end of a better understanding.
Life will always hold infinite possibility for us.

A wonderful note to end on today,
See you again tomorrow.

Dare2BU

Day 25 - Truth Comes With A Guarantee

Good morning

I love the infinite possibilities of life…
I love knowing that no matter what is going on for me, there is always more that's available.
That means when life is great it blows my mind that it's actually possible for it to be better. WOW!

And when life feels small and restrictive, when I'm feeling low and down, like I'm not enough or I've messed everything up and my head is spinning, I feel overwhelmed and like it's all too much for me I love knowing that all of that is just my experience in that moment, it's never truth.

I love knowing that I have enough resilience to always come back to balance, to always return to the truth of who I am.

You are exactly the same as me… you work exactly the same way. There's nothing that's available to me that's not available to you.

I love knowing that you have all the resilience you will ever need and that if you ever feel insecure, upset, lost, alone, scared or any of those sorts of things, you too have everything already within you to come back to balance. It is a given, it's within your make-up.

Human beings are wired for insight.
This is the way that we can access the truth of who we are that's beyond the words.
It's a built-in capacity we all have.

Sometimes we can feel as if we don't have insights, or not the really good ones, not the mind shattering and life changing ones.
But trust me you are always having insights, we all are.

There's nothing wrong with you, or different about you.
Be patient with yourself and you will begin to notice the changes that are happening for you.

We have often spent so many years with a very noisy mind that it's not always easy to notice the quieter, gentler, sounds of truth.
Keep going in this direction and believe me you will start to notice something.

I can't tell you exactly what you will see for yourself because Truth is universal. The amazing thing for you is that the implications of Truth are personal. They will be exactly what you need to have a life you love.

In the end if you will dare2bu, dare to look steadfastly in the direction of truth, then you can trust that your own personal resilience, excellence, oneness, and love will emerge from there.

That's guaranteed ~ that's the guarantee that comes with daring to look to truth.

So, keep going, you truly are onto something here.

Have a great day

Dare2BU

Day 26 - Why Would You Dare2BU?

I wanted to share with you why I am daring you to be you…

When we begin to look for ways to make life work for us, to find the peace and happiness that seems to be missing in our life it's very easy to come at it from believing that we already know the answer, we just have to find a way to implement it in our life.

But we have got it wrong ~ We really don't know.

Winston Churchill said 'men occasionally stumble over the truth, but most pick themselves up and carry on as if nothing happened'

The truth of who we are can at first sometimes be a very hard pill to swallow. It's way easier in the short term to turn away from it.

Because the truth is that it is our spiritual nature that is eternal and can never be damaged. The truth of who we are doesn't share the fate of our ego, our form or our body.

But we get very attached to this part of us, the ego, form, body, and mistakenly believe that it is who we really are and we want salvation for it. We don't want to let go of it, we hold on and we fight…sometimes very long and hard.

We keep on and on slogging to try and achieve this salvation, but it will never be reached this way it's impossible. All this ever does is ruin the pleasure we can have from being human.

When I dare you to be you, I am asking you to dare to let go of trying to find salvation for your body and your beliefs and the form of who you think you are because the way this works is the other way around. Find the truth of who you are and your human experience will be the very best it has ever been. Keep trying to improve your human experience from the outside and it will always fail at some point.

For centuries human beings have got it backwards.

We have been working really hard to try and make things right on the level of form when it simply will never ever work that way.
The way it works has become counter intuitive and most of us won't dare to take the chance and truly dare to be who we are.

Here's how it works.
When we nurture our spiritual nature, our humanness is already taken care of.

When we try to control things from our humanness we lose touch with our spiritual nature and the whole thing falls apart.

It can sometimes be very hard to trust that it works this way, there is an awful lot of evidence that seems to say it doesn't.

Dare2bu is an invitation to turn around and go in the right direction, the direction of truth and a daily reminder to keep doing this because it's very easy to forget and go back to old habits.

Over the next few days I'm going to be sharing with you some of the most common things that get in the way for us when we begin to change direction and how to continue to dare2bu!

Thank you for being here today
I love what we are doing together.
Have a wonderful day

Dare2BU

Day 27 - Why Do We Have To Suffer?

Hello again

One of the reasons we begin to look for ways to improve our life can be because we don't want bad things to happen, and when we come across the principles we are hoping that we have found a way to ensure that nothing bad happens in our life or to the people we love from now on.

It seems very unfair that innocent people have to suffer.

The thing with suffering is that when we are in the middle of it, in the heat of the moment, then nothing much will make sense to us. Yet as we get some distance or perspective things will look different to us. If you look back on any time you have suffered, you will see this is what happens.

I'm not saying this to belittle anyone's suffering or to make light of it, but to point out that all suffering is a product of our thoughts and level of understanding in that moment.

When we think about things from our past that we found traumatic we begin to suffer, when we don't think about those things or we allow ourselves to see them differently or our level of understanding is different then we feel different; the suffering is less.

It's not to say that these things didn't happen. It's to help us see that the thing changing when we suffer versus when we don't is our level of consciousness or understanding or our thought in the moment.

Another thing that many people often say about suffering is that whilst it was happening it was very difficult, and they wished things could be different but on reflection looking back it was this experience that helped them grow and become the person they are now, without going through this they wouldn't be so loving, connected or compassionate.

It is almost as if suffering is a part of the intelligence behind life, part of the greater plan for us that helps us to wake up to the truth of who we are.

The principles and this piece of writing are an explanation of how suffering occurs, not a thing you can do to stop you from suffering.

We suffer when we think that life works from the outside in, when we look outside to the world of form for the answers. Suffering eases when we realise that life works from the inside out and look within for answers.

We all do both of these things. Its human nature.

Understanding this somehow seems to help us to be way less interested in our wayward thoughts and asking why and going back over and over the same painful thoughts and this means we suffer less.

The more we orient to the truth of who we are, the more peace, love wisdom and connection there is in our life, the better our experience becomes. This always happens from the inside out.

Understanding gives us our best personal life experience available.

I hope this helps
Have a wonderful day

Dare2BU

Day 28 - Insight And Ultimate Truth

Hello again

We are here together talking about daring to be you...
looking to the truth of who you are so you can have the
best life experience available to you, a life you love.
When we decide to create a life of our dreams out in the
world there are often things that seem to get in our way.

Behind daring to be you is the hope that *you will* create a
life you love a life, doing way more of what you want to
be doing and far less of what you don't want to be doing.

To help you to move forward in this, the first thing that
comes to mind to talk to you about is insight.
You will find out who you truly are, and learn to know
and trust that to be true, via insight.

Everything I have been sharing and everything I will
continue to share is all great and very useful but
ultimately what will change things for you and what you
will truly gain from being in this conversation is what
you see for yourself through insight.

Insights aren't something rare, unusual or not available to
you, believe me you have been having them your whole
life.

They are as normal as breathing to all human beings. We don't always know exactly what an insight is and we can very easily miss our own. **But you will have had plenty.**

Until someone pointed out to you that you are breathing you probably didn't realise it, it was just something that went on for you pretty much unnoticed. Insights are the same, they have always been a part of your life but until pointed out they have probably mostly gone unnoticed.

An insight is inner wisdom revealing itself to us. It's that moment when we realise we know something, that ah-ha moment, or maybe a 'doh!!...how did I miss that?' moment. Something reveals itself to us that once seen we can hardly believe we didn't see it before. Insights can be earth shattering or a quiet, barely noticeable shift and anything in-between.

It is called insight because it has revealed itself from within… it didn't come from the outside, even if it was sparked by something outside. Like maybe reading this book. Insight always and only ever comes to you from you, it's personal and it benefits you.

So, stop listening for and analysing information and start listening for insight. Information, although useful, is not where the magic is in all of this, what comes from within you is what you will keep and what will transform your life.

The second thing I would like to suggest is that begin to listen for ultimate truth - stop defending what you believe to be true and what you think might help you..
Ultimate truth is the same for everyone but its benefits are personal to the one hearing it in that moment.

This can be hard sometimes.

When we have believed something to be true for a long time we may have a lot invested in it staying true for us. And as we begin to hear ultimate truth it can threaten the things we hold in this way. We can be sorely tempted to listen for ways to help us stay where we are.

Even though it may be of huge benefit to hear ultimate truth and allow it to work it's magic through us there can be things we fight to keep the way they are that get in the way of reaping those benefits as we move forward in life.

So, to end for today I want to invite you to get curious about insights and ultimate truth… no analysis or over thinking, just leave it to simmer on the backburner of your mind.

Have a fun and fabulous day,
Can't wait to see you again tomorrow....

Dare2BU

Day 29 – Fun, Games And Creation

Hello again

I cannot believe we have reached day 29 already. Thank you for being here with me I really appreciate it.

I love writing this book each day, it's something that works for me - writing in this way.
I love sharing what I can see and hope you are having insights and shifts as you read.
I love that all these things are happening.

My life has changed beyond recognition from what it was just a few short years ago, in a very good way. Even after I came across the principles I simply never realised it was possible to have a life this good. That came a little bit later, since I've had this realisation one of my favourite things to do is play with life and the creative process…to dare2bme!

It used to look to me as if there were a lot of things in the world that made it either difficult or impossible for me to have a life that I love.

The more I see what's possible for me, and I know that you and I absolutely work in the same way, the more I know that you can have a life that works for you too. A life you truly love, one that you may not even have dared to think was possible in the past.

So, are you ready to have some fun and see what's possible for you?
If you are then let's play this game together and see just how good life can be.

There are essentially only two questions that we ever need to ask of ourselves as we begin to dare2b who we truly are and have more of what we want in our life.

The first question is:
What is it you want to create in your life?

The second question is:
What stops you from just doing it?

So, for today, I would love you to look at these questions and if you want to get a pencil and paper and make a few notes then please do so.

First of all, start to let your mind play with what you would like to create in the world… if your life was exactly how you would like it to be what would it look like?

What does a happy successful life look like to you?

Think of or write down up to three things you would really love to create, things that would look like success to you and you would love to be doing.

Then when you have done that look at the second
question…

What stops you from just doing it?

What are the biggest things that seem to be in the way of
you creating the success you would like to have out in the
world?

Have some fun with this, play full out. Don't hold back
it's a great game.

I would love to help as many people as possible to realise
their full potential and I want to create ways to do this
that also support me.
I have already started with this one, you being here and
reading this is a part of it.

Have lots of fun, until tomorrow....

Dare2BU

Day 30 - Life Is Weighted In Your Favour

Hello again

I'm really excited to be here today, how did you get on with the questions yesterday??

I have to confess to this not being new to me and I have great fun every time.
The first time I played this game I was very cautious and I didn't let myself really go for it. I stayed within very reasonable boundaries and only allowed myself to think about things that seemed possible.

Each time I play now, I really get into it and let myself just have great fun.
I think about some really 'out there things I might like.
Then I let that all just be there and after a while a couple of things choose themselves for me to go for!

If you need more time then that's fine, if you already know what you would like that's fine too.

Let's move on. But do remember you can take all the time you need and you can come back here as many times as you like.

For most of the first half of our time together we have been looking at who you truly are, and what that means for you in your life here as a human being.

I'd like to sum that up for you now, so you can see when you start to create anything you want in life what you have going for you and what might get in your way.

You are the creative essence of the universe, the way that shows up for us is that we always get what we need in the moment.

In a similar way to a Sat Nav that gives you the next turn to take in the road, the intelligence that is working through you will always give you exactly what you need in the moment you need it.

And just like a Sat Nav if you don't listen to what it tells you it just works out where you are and gives you the next best step from there.

It never gets annoyed with you or gives up on you, no matter how many times you decide not to listen and how ever far away from where you are headed you get, it just calmly recalculates and gives you your next best step. This is a fabulous thing to have in your corner.

In my experience when we set out to do something in the world, sometimes it works and sometimes it doesn't.

So long as you remember that your okay-ness is never dependent on anything working out the way you think it should you are fine to play full out and just keep taking the next step.

You may not always end up where you planned to be, but you will have a lot of fun and you can never lose anything that you truly need.

Your okay-ness, your security and your freedom are innate and will always be yours no matter what.
This is another amazing thing to have going for you.

You are human, so your body has limitations.
As a human being we do have physical limitations.

It's a good thing to eat and sleep. It's a good thing to look after yourself.
So long as you remember this and follow that Sat Nav this shouldn't be a problem.

We are human, but that is what enables us to have this experience, so it's accounted for as long as we remember all the things we have going in our favour.

So hopefully now you have decided to have some fun and create a life you love out in the world.

Now you have been reminded of what you have going for you, over the next few days we will look a little more closely at what can get in your way…

Have a lovely day.

Dare2BU

139

Part Four;

Dare2BU

Day 31 - Understanding And Information

Good morning

I hope you are having a good day?

When I first came across the principles and I knew I wanted to start working with people teaching them about how this understanding transforms lives I was most certainly not grounded enough.
I had had some insights but I absolutely didn't know enough to share it with others in an impactful way.

When I tried with my friends and family, as soon as someone was in front of me, getting upset about what appeared to be a horrible circumstance that was causing them to feel the way they did, I was lost.

What they were saying seemed real and true to me. It seemed perfectly reasonable to feel the way they did and very much as if their feelings were coming from what was going on for them in the world around them.

I lacked knowledge and I lacked understanding.

I would get very down and feel as if this was something that was getting in the way of me reaching my dreams.

I would often feel hopeless and cross with myself.

Then I had the realisation that this was perfectly normal. I was trying to run before I could walk.

Things happen on God's time not on mine.

All I had to do was take the next step and see that I am always taken care of no matter what is going on. I always have what I need in any given moment, but I am also capable of creating a very believable illusion that I am in control and things are not working out as they should be.

I was being caught in the very trap I was trying to help others avoid.

If one of the things that gets in the way of you creating what you want in the world is that you don't have enough understanding or information don't get annoyed or frustrated, look for a way to fill that gap.

Google might even be a great place to start.
There might well be some very practical steps you can take to find out what it is you don't know.

Once I just allowed myself the time I needed (and that wasn't determined by me) this problem resolved itself.

Sometimes it's that simple. We just don't always see it.

Have a wonderful day

Debra Simmons

Day 32 - Am I Alright Even Here?

Good morning.

I hope you are well and having a good day.
Whilst writing this chapter, I had a sore throat and a cough.

What I noticed was that it was way less of an inconvenience than it would have been in the past. I am seeing more and more places where no matter what is going on I am okay and nothing can change that.

I'm not saying I wasn't poorly, I'm saying that with less thinking about it life is just way less complicated and seems to have a habit of working itself out.

When I realised that I needed a deeper understanding and more information I found ways to sort that out, but it seemed there were still other things getting in the way of me having a life I loved…

One of them was clearly thought I was having that looked like truth.

The thing with thoughts that look like truth is that they don't appear to be thoughts at all. We see them as truth before we have any thought about them.

Then we listen to them and they have us doing, or not doing, all sorts of things that limit what we can, or can't, or will, or won't, do in our lives.

For example, when I *believed* my anxious thoughts about driving it meant I was very limited as to where I could go by car.

And here's the thing, I can still have anxious thinking, but what I have seen is that it doesn't make one jot of difference to what I am capable of...

- ⅄ I can still drive
- ⅄ I can still go places

It seems to me now these anxious thoughts have no idea whose head they have appeared in. They've got the wrong person if they want to stop me driving or doing a whole host of other things that I can have anxious thoughts about.
With, or without, anxious thoughts the truth of who I am never changes.

I have seen that anxious thinking is a human thing not a circumstance thing.

When I take a lot of notice of it and allow it to control my life then it does just that, more and more 'things' appear to cause me to feel anxious.

146

When I just let it be there and know that it can't hurt me, or change who I am, I seem to have way less anxious thinking.

The thing with feeling anxious is it has nothing to do with driving, or walking into a room full of people, or talking in front of a group, or any of the other million things we can attach it to.

It has everything to do with our thinking in the moment and absolutely nothing else.
Once we begin to see that we never have to be scared of our own thinking then anything can be going on in our mind and we are home and dry.

We are taken care of and no matter what happens our okay-ness always remains intact.

Because, beyond all that thinking is our connection to Mind…or the creative essence of who we are, or new thought, new ideas, freedom, peace and love.

The more we live our lives from this connection then the more likely we are to create wonderful things and have a life filled with all the things that mean the most to us.

Once we can see past the thoughts that keep us small we can see more of the creative intelligence of the universe showing up for us in ways we could never have thought were possible before.

I have something I would love you to play around with over the next few days...
Look beneath the thinking you are having in the moment to see what's there for you.

For me that looks a bit like this.
When my thinking goes crazy I ask myself the question

'Am I alright even here?'

It seems to me the answer is always yes.

It was doing this that enabled me to do the longest zip
wire in Europe in 2016. It is also the reason I am
confident I can attempt a sky dive in the near future. Even
though heights are one of the scariest things for me.

Because this is how I play the game of life, it's how I see
thought for what it is and how I challenge it and have a
way better life because of what I see when I do that.

You don't have to do a zip wire or a sky dive, but I would
invite you to see what thought stops you from doing and
creating in your life that would be fun and a great
experience for you.

Have a fabulous day
See you again tomorrow!

Dare2BU

Day 33 - Nothing Changes Truth

Hello....

I would love to expand a bit on 'Am I alright even here?'

Right now, in this moment as I am typing this chapter my sore throat has gotten much worse. My eyes are sore and I'm not feeling great.

Very gently I'm asking myself the question 'Am I alright even here?'

And, as always, the answer is YES.

When I connect to that knowing within me then I am capable of way more than I knew I was. And my experience of this illness is very different to what it would have been before I understood the truth of who I am.

Do I feel ill? Yes.
Does it bother me in the way it would have done in the past? No.

I want to be clear this isn't about making myself do things I am too ill to do or not listening to my body when it's telling me to rest.

What I want to share is that I haven't found anywhere that I am not ok. In my experience there is nowhere that is possible. There is nowhere where we are not taken care of, there is no experience that can affect or change the truth of who we are.

Our salvation lies in seeing that truth. The simple question 'Am I alright even here?', when we ask it for our self and look within for the answer it uncovers that truth for us, it reveals it so we can see it.

We either see this through understanding and daring to hear our inner voice or we miss it because it's hidden by thought in the moment.

When we see it, our felt experience is lighter and easier and happier and healthier. When we don't our felt experience can be heavy, and we can struggle.

I invite you to keep playing with
'Am I alright even here?'

Have a great day....

Debra Simmons

Day 34 - I'm Not Good Enough

Hello again...

Oh my! this one been a biggy for me.... believing I'm not good enough. For a very long time it plagued my life.

How about you? Have you ever felt as if everyone else has something you don't and that you will just never measure up?

Has this ever stopped you from doing things you would love to do in the world? It certainly has me.

It stopped me driving, it stopped me phoning my friends, it stopped me asking for things I needed, like help and money when I worked for others. It had me killing myself cleaning my house, so nobody could possibly think I was incapable. And a lot more besides. It had me on the run, wearing myself out trying to get everything right.

Boy, was I on the wrong track.
As human beings we are judging machines, it's what we do.

We assess and judge everything, most of the time without even being aware we are doing it. We are very often the harshest on our self.

When I was feeling insecure I would look at other people and it would seem as if they were prettier, or cleverer, or thinner or younger than I was.

It would look as if they had more money than I did or way better opportunities than I ever had. Some people seemed to have it all, while I appeared to have nothing. The world seemed like a very unfair place and I had the booby prize.

Have you ever felt some version of that?

What I have seen is that I can't change or control my thoughts, if those thoughts are going to come then they are going to come. But if I understand the nature of thought, just because all of that is in my head it doesn't mean it's real or true…

Here's a thought.

What if you can have all of that insecure thinking and you are still perfectly good enough?
In fact, what if you are better than good enough? What if you are the creative essence of the universe and none of that thinking means a thing??

Oh yes! You are the creative essence of the universe, you can just let your thinking do whatever it wants, it can't change the truth of who you are, it can't hurt you and it can't stop you being awesome.

154

Every human being has the capacity to see the truth of this and that is where our peace and happiness lie.

I could easily have let the story "I am not good enough because I am unwell" get in the way of me writing this chapter and just being me.
It has crossed my mind, but I'm really not interested in that thinking.

It's not that I never fall for my wayward thinking in the moment, I sometimes do. But I am very lucky to have this conversation be so big a part of my life that it doesn't take long before truth has shone it's light onto the path and I'm back to peace and understanding.

The more I keep myself looking in this direction, the more it seems that my thinking changes of it's own accord and when it doesn't I really don't give a monkeys!

I invite you to be both suspicious and curious about your thinking.
Once we take our thinking to be true we are lost for a while. As soon as we are suspicious or curious then we are already finding our way back.

Have a brilliant day, let thought do what it likes…
You are always ok...

Debra Simmons

Day 35 - Other People

Good Morning.

Other people….oh my can it look to me as if other people are the cause of my upset and pain. Equally it can look as if they bring me the biggest amount of love and pleasure. I am eternally grateful that I know the truth.

In the past, other people have been high on my list of things that looked like they stopped me doing what I wanted to do in my life. At times it's even looked as if they have really messed my life up. I wasted a lot of time believing that to be true.

I always wanted all the love and good feelings it seemed I got from other people, but I didn't want any of the pain.

- I didn't want to feel lonely
- I didn't want to feel that people didn't like me
- I didn't want to be bullied or picked on

I think for most of us, until we come across this particular understanding, it is pretty much a given that our feelings can be caused by other people. It is the way most people believe life works.
It's stated in most love songs and taken as true by most of us most of the time.

It came as quite a surprise to me when I realised the truth is that **it's not other people that cause my feelings….EVER!**

My feelings always and only ever come from the creative intelligence behind the universe, or God, or Mind. Life always works from the inside out.

I am not here as something stand alone and separate from everything, or even *anything,* around me and fighting against things will only keep the world the way it is, in disarray, discontentment and deeply suffering.

I can't say I always see that when I look out at the world going on around me, but I do know that it's always true.

Insightfully knowing is enough.

Until you know that other people can't ever be the cause of how you feel, it will look like it's a good idea to try and change them, or yourself, somehow.

You might try and discredit them, or plead with them, or fight against them or avoid them. You might try and change your own behaviour in an attempt to make theirs different.

It will look like they, or you, are broken or wrong somehow.
All of this is pointless, exhausting and ineffective.
It is not where real and lasting change occurs.

We run ourselves ragged trying to make something work in a way it simply never will.

I want to orient you to the truth once again as that is the most helpful thing to anyone. This is where ease and effective change happen naturally.

There is something about the system that you have been born into that is very helpful for you to know;

It's on your side, it's there to help you, to look after you and to nurture you.

What's more, it is always doing all of those things even if you don't know it.

Once you begin to see the truth of who you are, other people can't possibly be a problem. Because a by-product of orienting towards truth is that your own love and connection and resilience begin to emerge.

Trusting the system and going with it will have you feeling all the love and connection you could ever wish for.

As this happens any answers that you need to help you navigate the world and the people in it will naturally come to you. You will find that this system looks after you in ways beyond anything you thought was possible.

So, let yourself have a great and creative day...

Debra Simmons

Day 36 - You Are Built For Insight

Hello again...

It's a great day for an insight!

We have already touched upon insight but I didn't want these forty days to end without expanding on this subject at least a little bit.
Not least because it's just so mind-blowingly great how we are all built for insight and what that means for you and your learning.

I have said before that truth is the same for every one of us.
Truth isn't any different for you than it is for me.
There is a way in which we are all connected and in which we are all the same. That is truth.
Then we have our uniqueness…the place where we are individual. Where we have our own personal life experience. The illusion of separation. Our human life.

When we start to look in the direction of truth ~ which is what we are doing together here ~ What occurs to us will be helpful to us personally in our ordinary daily life.
That's the gift of insight.

161

Because insight *is* what will occur to us.
And it is our best way to have the best life experience
available.

As human beings we don't come with everything we
need fully developed, but we come with the capacity to
develop everything we need. That's part of the fun. We
can learn.

Like an acorn that holds everything it will need to
become a mighty oak, we have within us everything we
need to become the very best version of us.
Insight is the gift by which we learn things beyond our
mind.

We gain insight into the things we are interested in.
It's a human trait.
If we put our attention onto something we will naturally
learn more about it.

Just because you are here, paying attention to this, you
will begin to have insights about your own true nature
that are helpful to you personally.

That's what I find so mind-blowingly fabulous about this
system we are all a part of, it takes care of us in ways we
could never make happen on our own if we were truly
individual and alone.

What occurs for you, and to you, is yours. It's most
helpful to you and it's just what you need in the moment
it occurs to you. It is responsive, and it adapts to you and
your needs as you grow and change.

It's never out of date and it never comes before you are ready.

Its brilliant to be in this conversation it's so helpful to us. Collaboration and sharing truth brings out the best in us all, and it's a really helpful way to spark all of this from within.

Because that's where it always comes from, within, it was always already there. It was always yours. Nobody gives this to you, it's only possible to waken to what you already are.

It's not possible to reach the end of insight either.
No matter how good this all gets the possibility for more is no less now than it was the first time you ever realised anything for yourself.
However much you see there will always be more.

You and I are truly blessed to have been born into such a system with the ability to learn and to know about it.

I'm not sure if I always fully realise just what I have found. It is the most profound and precious thing. I am glad that I can share it with you.

Have a wonderful day
Feeling very humble and blessed.

Debra Simmons

Day 37 - Money

Hello...

Has it ever appeared that money has stopped you doing things you want to do out in the world?

It has me.
Money seems to be one of those things that for so many of us it really looks as if it has some kind of power over us.

We give it a hugely elevated status.

I could write a whole forty days just on the subject of money (maybe I will very soon).

When I came across the principles, money was the only place in my life that I didn't seem to be able to come unstuck.

Lots of other things fell away and looked different, but money, that was my block.
It has only been fairly recently that I have seen through my own thinking about it.

Wow it is so liberating. I have been waiting for the chance to share this one with you.

165

We have lots of myths about money that look very real and true, but as usual when we shine the light of truth onto them they don't stand up.

A big one is that money gives us security.
This is simply not true.
There is no amount of money that gives you security.
I remember first realising this when Russ, my partner, and I were visiting with some friends who are a fair bit better off than we are.

They had just bought a new house and we went to see it.
What a beautiful house it was too.
On the way driving over Russ and I were discussing that if we just had the money our friends had we would be fine.

We didn't have quite enough, but what they had was perfect. We were certain they had just the right amount.

The funny thing was they didn't think that.

They had pushed themselves to their limit to buy this house and while we were talking with them they were complaining that if only they had just a relatively small chunk more they would be fine. They were just a small chunk short...

It was during this conversation I really saw, there is quite simply no magic amount of money that is enough. Money doesn't work that way.

Money is a useful tool, but it won't give you security or freedom or love or happiness or peace of mind.

All of these things are already ours, they are built into the system.
See this and if you want to you will be able to create all the money you want. Miss it and money will evade you.

Yesterday when I talked about the fact that we are born with everything we need within us, one of those things is the ability to learn. And we have access to our own inner guidance system; the creative potential of the universe (Mind or God).
Between these things we have everything we could ever need to have a life beyond anything we could imagine.

It never ceases to amaze me what we miss.

When I first came across the principles I was listening to a recording George Pransky had made, he was talking about a client who had lost his job and was feeling very depressed and down.

He came to see George and during a conversation his mind cleared and he realised he had access to money he had forgotten he had.
When I listened to this I thought, well it's alright for him he has a pot of money…. I don't… it's different for me.

My latest insight around money has shown me where I do in fact have access to money I never saw I had. Even back when I was listening to that recording it was there just waiting for me to be open minded enough to see it. I keep marvelling at that, I hardly believe it myself some days.

I'm not sure if your block is, like mine, a money
one…but I do know this;
Whatever you are seeing with eyes that tell you that you
lack something, or that you are different to everyone else,
it's alright for them and it's not for you, believe me your
mind is not clear enough for you to see just how rich you
are.
You are simply misunderstanding something, stay in this
conversation, there is magic available here beyond
anything money can buy.

Have a wonderful rich day,
Heaps of love

Dare2BU

Day 38 - A Short Sweet Reminder

Hello again...

Over the last few days we have been looking at all sorts of things that can look real to us when we decide to create something out in the world. Things that appear to get in our way and stop us in our tracks.

When something looks like it has the power to stop us in our tracks there is only one thing that can be happening**, we are forgetting how we work and the truth of who we are.**

When I was a small child my granddad had a joke he would sometimes share.
He would say
'If someone asks you for directions…scratch your head and say'…
"If I was going there, I wouldn't start from here"

The thing is the only place we can ever start from is exactly where we are right now in this moment because all we ever have is this moment.
It will truly benefit you to remember that this moment always contains everything we will ever need in it.

To do what is needed in any given moment we don't need more confidence or to be better than we are or to have more money or more knowledge or a more positive mind-set, or to be different in any way at all.

It is very easy to believe our mind when it tells us that we do.

I wanted to take just a few minutes of your time today to remind you that you don't need anything other than what you have in this moment. Read it slowly, take it in then stop for a second and remember

When something looks like it has the power to stop us in our tracks there is only one thing that can be happening, we are forgetting how we work and the truth of who we are.

I hope you know just how amazing and how blessed you are.
Have a great day...

Debra Simmons

Day 39 - Enjoy The View.

Good morning...

How are you doing?
I hope yesterday's short sweet reminder awakened
something in you that reminded you how you work and
about the truth of who you are.

Every day, this whole time we have been together, I have
been pointing you towards these two things.

How we work and the truth of who you are.

I've been doing this because it is always and only ever
misunderstanding these things that causes us pain and
suffering.
As soon as we see the truth again the suffering subsides.

We work from the inside out. We project what we see out
in the world from within. There is not an objective world
'out there' and then we see it from different points of
view. There is no world until we project it from within
us.

Our projection of it changes as we remember or forget the
truth of how it works.
There are good reasons to stay in this conversation.

173

It is perfectly normal to forget, to get caught up in our own projection. We all do it. Then we remember again. The more familiar we are with the truth the less completely we forget and when we do the sooner we remember again.
Staying in the conversation helps you to remember.

I recall an occasion when I went for a walk, with a friend who was staying with me. I often walk and it's very hilly where I live in North Devon, I am used to going up and down some pretty steep inclines. My friend lives in a much flatter place.
When we got to the top of a particularly steep hill we were both panting and struggling for breath.
Within a few seconds I got my breath back, she took much longer and was glad when we were finished walking.

My body is used to this kind of walking and although I get out of breath I recover pretty quickly.
My friend is not so used to it and she took much longer to return to 'normal'.

I am aware how my mind works, I'm used to my thinking misleading me, and it gets back to truth pretty quickly.
My recovery time is way shorter than it used to be.
The more I stay in the conversation the more easily I recover when I get into some wayward thinking.

Some 'thought hills' are tougher than others but being 'fit' in this way is a massive help.
Staying in the conversation is like exercising, it's a great way to keep your mind fit and healthy and used to looking towards truth when things get a little tricky.

The more we understand our own mind and what it does, the more we can be out in the world having fun and living a life we love.

It's not that life won't continue to be life, it will. There will always be hills to climb, but if we are fit and healthy then we will take them in our stride and enjoy all the beautiful scenery from some of those amazing high vantage points.

Have a fabulous day.

Debra Simmons

Day 40 - Let's Not End This Here

Hello for our last day together...

I cannot believe we have already been here together for 40 days…time goes so quickly when you are enjoying yourself. I have really loved sharing what I see with you. I hope it has been helpful to you.

I really believe that staying in this conversation or continuing to look in this direction is immeasurably helpful in all of our lives.
I love the idea that there will be a time when we are all operating out in the world with an understanding of how we work.

This way when we fall under the spell of believing and listening to our own wayward thinking in the moment our fellow human beings will be there to remind us of what is happening and help point us swiftly back towards the truth. Every time I think that my life can't get any better and that I must have had the insight to blow all others out of the water, I see something more deeply and I see more of what is possible for me.

177

I'd love for you to continue to experience more of what is possible for you.
I'd love to watch you continue to grow and expand, create and learn.

Mind, which is always running through you, is the space of all possibility.

And, finally, I will leave you with this reminder:

It turns out you are a part of the creative essence of this entire universe. There are simply no limits on that and no limits on you.

Dare2BU

About the Author

Debra Simmons came across a spiritual understanding in 2011 which changed her life in a really great way.
It continues to have an impact on her every day as she gets a clearer and deeper understanding of who she is and how life works.
Based on 3 simple principles this understanding challenges many of our every-day assumptions, making it easy to learn but hard to master.
Debra has a team, Dare2BU, who work together to run retreats, talks, workshops and other events to help people find a more fulfilling and contented way of living.
To find out more about Debra, and the team, visit www.DebraSimmons.co.uk or follow DebraSimmons.co.uk on Facebook
If you have enjoyed this book you can join Debra's Facebook group *"Here & Now"* to keep in this conversation.

Debra Simmons

Printed in Great Britain
by Amazon